Echoes in Still Air

poems by

Diana Athena

Finishing Line Press
Georgetown, Kentucky

Echoes in Still Air

*I dedicate this collection to Nicole Hudson,
in memory of Maclyn Reed.*

ACKNOWLEDGMENTS

Thank you to Finishing Line Press for giving a home to this collection. Thank
you to Edwin Torres, Lynn Xu, Joshua Edwards, Emily Skillings, and Grace
Patt Biddle for reading the manuscript in the early stages and providing
valuable feedback. A huge thank you to Matthew Burgess and Bert Eisenstadt
for their mentorship and guidance through the years. Thank you to Victor
Dizon, Ariana Rosen, Gina Rizzi, and Tasha Jakush for their friendship and
for always reading my poems as I continued to develop my craft. Thank you
to all my teachers and friends who helped me become the person and the
writer I am today. Thank you to Sophie Kautenburger for the cover art. Special
thank you to Patricio Hernández for always believing in me and supporting
my ambitions.

Publisher: Leah Huete de Maines
Editor: Christen Kincaid
Cover Art: Sophie Ellen Kautenburger
Author Photo: Patricio Hernández Palazuelos
Cover Design: Elizabeth Maines McCleavy

Order online: www.finishinglinepress.com
also available on amazon.com

Author inquiries and mail orders:
Finishing Line Press
PO Box 1626
Georgetown, Kentucky 40324
USA

Contents

at the breaking point 1

where the whales fall 11

there are no trees outside of poetry 21

Before I organise myself, I must disorganize myself internally.

—Clarice Lispector, *Agua Viva*
(translated by Stefan Tobler)

/ /

The letters are breaking formation,
the last
dreamproof skiffs—

—Paul Celan, *Breathturn*
(translated by Pierre Joris)

at the breaking point

too are made of mud / and if you let her
the earth / will hold you

mist envelops / suspends all
movement—smoldering / the birchwood melody

      / release your salt—your skin shed

sweetgrass / smudging over heat
giving stones / unity of soil and prayer

      / bow your head—thoughts
         fall to dust—each direction / east   north /
                                / you   now /

uttering of briar / when the last
note sleeps / atman hears

      / kneel—the body
         that became too heavy—you

rearranged in the pattern of fulfillment / no plot
but touch infused with luster / with trust

                              / no longer in my body
              / a stream under the stones

tender feet /   / inhale
each pebble / each twig / each frail leaf

uncovered in solitude

moths rest with wings open / waiting to be discovered
swaying with spells / breaking /   / the rhythm

of aspiration / anticipating / words crowd—
withdraw / drown with sudden indifference

        crave subtlety / no words / but breath

navy petals are bells
/ relax into their music

string the moments—
a mixture of burgundy

/ gold at the end
of a serpentine road

nocturnal aquamarine
spills over the furrowed ocean

/ an aura of a migraine

/ where sorrow
covers the landscape

/ a fountain deprived of water
by the earthquake

/ louder when the voice sounds

silence / all I hear

I enter language /

at the breaking /   / point

steel /   / corroded

tender flashes /   / thunder

the sound /   / a storm

my fragile body /   / landing

on the windowsill /   / replaying

/ the leap year

un / done is an antecedent   to rearranged
   solved / to the beat   of the running shoes

stitched by the silver   threads of freshwater
   slipping through the sutures   of perspective
      adding a touch of chartreuse   to mature pine

the horizon is soundless   edges sewn together
   with a moving thread   looping between the surface
      and the sky   in carefree stitches

caressing the polyester   with irascible upward
   strokes defying the laws   of gravity / pulling
      images out the pores   of my mortality and into

somber streams / merging   with rubber soles
   the streetlights mumble   in the steady rain

      a lightbulb stumbles   once / gives in and settles
into frequency   flickering to the rhythm

   of the feet splashing   through stubborn water
      chipping / at the limestone   formations / rancor

pouring out of my body   into the spring / with each
   step / with each drop   beseeching the feet
      to be broken into particles   parted / at the seams

/ still here /

behind the keys / fingers chase
/ black & white / two sides / space filled

/ the underwater /

an orchid bud where   each petal is a boundary
          between   the blueprint and
     vitality blooming   with every move
I no longer want   I remain present / choose to
greet you / with ecstasy   unzip the outer shell
          instead of glitter   bathe in
hot pink / translucent   coral / instead of offering
     to prove my worth   I choose to see you
          free of ornament   practice being
     witness the ego   with tenderness
one is a pirouette / betrayal   another is the sound of Aum
          transcending   one is immediate
     a gasp devouring   mature leaves in gusts—
          the other is / the breath   traceable
in concentration / steadily   lungs fill / with fragrance
     ribcage weaves peonies   collarbones part intoxicated
          with fulfillment /   that evening I come home
          to hold you—   find empty shelves
     my tongue is fastened   inside of the illusion
          where functional   doesn't mean capable
     I try to fit myself   inside a flask for months
          then break   you never learn sobriety
means remembrance   not void / she is abundance

my skin unattended / a braid
    of empty spaces /
                / fused
with the color of depression

                / where last spring is
                / whited out
                / where I mourn once

where the whales fall

where everything has already happened
where I have / no right to choose

seal the lips / path
of resistance / safety of habit /

soften the eyelids / pupils narrow
to resemble the flame / dancing / in captivity

/ exhale / stillness is a choice

pooled in waxed crater a mirror
surface / a tarn spilled over

/ the movement of inner currents—is water
restrained by its depth / fluidity of flame

the now / deeper into the past—deeper—
where death is a narrative—deeper—

a shape /
a shape / a shape /

/ a sh
/ shape
/ un / shaped

underwater / rays
break

submerged / I look up /
the sky / now silver

above my head /
rains backwards / up and up /

air / caged in liquid
a shape / globe-like

contours blur /
/ up and up
air /

the eight ball on the break / stricken / crossed out
under the widow's veil /
                                          / a leap year
is framed in blackwood / holding a life

that no longer wants to be held / upright
as an upside-down moon

/ exhale /
calming / the cave's ribcage /

onyx / below limestone tombs /
where the whales fall fins of the heartbeat fade /

black ink / a smooth line /
behind the sun the sea is amber /

the moonlight / is a crevice
in the mirror of stone / one step / two

/ spaces are written
into the curtain of water /
/ everything falls

melted droplets / spilled paint /
desire not trusted /

misplaced emerald
/ blink /
fill palms with green luster / sew
apertures with vines / peonies in cavities
/ roots / years smoldering / corroding
/ each petal / unbraid
/ my life /   / no longer two /
walk into a stream / lay motionless /
validity starts to peel / hold breeze
tightly in your air / fingers / amethysts / pure /
not sure before the touch / slip
through a melody
/ linger /
through the air

watermelon pink / milky
apricot / pastel turquoise

        lavender blush / periwinkle
        lemongrass brightened

                with specks of honey:
                colors descend in waves
of pleasure / kiss
my skin—brief
        touches / pecks almost—leave
        sunshine in the dips
                of cheeks / corners
                lifted / the art is drifting /
away from the frames
pulled with binding

        threads / the shore always invites
        lost objects: a hair clip
                slipped in the deep
                sea a lifetime ago
a flip flop washed away
by the high tide two
        summers back / a cigarette
        carelessly tossed
                into the waves
                too warm for this
winter mouth
        year after year
        the label faded but
                elsewhere still clinging
where notes combine—each is
        enough while holding on

memories miles up /
into the sky / out
  into another dimension

      / the eruption
meant to warn
  mouths open
         unhinged / unbalanced /
         across the sound / tongue
         washed out /
in awe / irises mesmerized /
inevitability of never

        bits of barbed wire
        swallowed / clawed
         into a yarn / the throat
                 a steady consuming light
       is split / pieces of magma /
       edges uneven / searching
              where droplets / break
                common sense
      for concealed gaps / slipping
      into the unity of chaos / insert
       random vowels
             glimmering morning
             dew / no need to balance
              the voltage

             boundaries drip /
             admit life / at the end
              of this body is another

monsoon season / rainy gray
water breaks against

the eighth floor window
(that eventually might become mine

again) / sings in low
pitches / sparks

a metaphysical harmony
as I watch this short lived

reign / corals grow in the body
frightened to melt into

softness / convinced life

doesn't belong in the solitary
intent—I have spent

too many years praying
while my strength

kept peeling off in thick
layers from the lack

of bonds / a pearl white
branch drained of color

among empty shells / exploited
in the marathon of more—

my body deprived
of love / ready

there are no trees
outside of poetry

body holds / breath
unfolds silhouettes / the sky

softened the night / two shores
bridged by moonlight—now and

then—an opening / let the mist
dress your skin

/ immersed in being
feel / every drop /
                                    / the weightless fabric
between what is / the years pass
swirl / erase the contour—dancing

water is made of color—
where the mind can't knot

into pastel shades / spring

mourning / hold my breath
into the new moon

                             / water the soil
my body / spoiled

             / life wilted

like a painting in direct sun—
leaves faded

a yellow shade / an invisible plane
suspended /

      / one inch closer
            / concealed incantation

an embroidery / within the cerulean canvas
from the long passed rain

so gentle /   / still

few steps aside / soft spikes
not yet ready to kindle

/ a presence

/ an incident

when inspiration grasps
                              / the hands stop

/ hang in between the hours

hold / steady
breathing / the next inhale

witness / the nature
of the proper name

          / what if I stays I
          / ungoverned

in the absence
of gravity

Rahu is a ravenous planet / serpent feeding / never filled / tangled in knots / cursive / each intersection / a promise / chance to wrap a thread around the knuckle / an itching thought / again / a karmic wheel / irrational spokes / throat burns / wildfires / two bodies / drawing the veil / lifetimes / inquiries suspended / unmapped / intertwined / I am the mist / wrapping each branch / each curve / a lifelong task / fulfilled in longing / as the breath rushes to hold / stillness / air / fuel / heat / caresses dry logs / I hold your breath with the open palm / surrender my body to your voice / fill my emptiness with long sentences / tease / lack meaning / roll your tongue in cascades of sound crushing against skin / a chain of blinding bursts / in the chiming between shutter and rapture / caught on film / in stolen line breaks / in softness of my wrist / evaporate through sunrise dew / between now and the pit of samsara / in tenderness of almost touch / aspiration / the skin / velvet filled with purr / Ketu remains a headless shadow / blooms silk petals / I press my lips against your back / sip the words

/ blue is no longer / blue /
    milk at boiling temperature /
    sips of the sky

    / water and fire / same force
    / ash and foam / two shades

air is louder when walls are heard / dust densely folds
/ in bone / the sound
watercolor on canvas / fading / indigo of central time
/ paint
cascades / drowning / in liquid fabric / melted

the way hair melts caught on fire / dusk coats the city
/ touch / the pit
the voice has kindled / spring in my words
/ meld
desire too short to capture on film / rewind

leading all questions up / enchanted irises
imprinted into softness I / am no longer I
but we / breathing time swelled like a storm bud

the sun
/ above /

sweat / the ground
pray / the mud
   / loved /

burn / the stars
taste /

moth / essence of vetiver

/ intuition /   / an utterance
/ a palm /   / sprouts
writing /   / somehow easier

on scraps / scattered to / gether
barefoot / on the hardwood floor

feel /   / to give up thinking /
past is un / done / incoherent

paper / attention of a vivid
love /   / memoir scaffolds / searching

your scent / spring earth / silver
stitches of fertility / wings of a luna

Born in Omsk, Russia, **Diana Athena** started to develop an interest in writing as a teenager, writing poems and song lyrics in Russian. However, after moving to the United States at the age of nineteen, it took her eight years to rediscover her old passion and to start writing in English.

Diana's writing is often inspired by her yoga and meditation practice and explores language alongside breath. Her poems stop and illuminate time inviting the reader to confront their own interiority against the outer limits of the body. Diana's poems have received the Beatrice Dubin Rose and Bernard Grebanier Awards and appeared in *The Junction Journal, The Lit, Stuck in the Library,* and *Ghost Girls Zine.*

Diana received her BFA from Brooklyn College, CUNY, and a Creative Writing MFA from Columbia University. Outside of writing, Diana works as a yoga instructor and as a creative writing teacher at various levels. This is her first poetry collection.

www.ingramcontent.com/pod-product-compliance
Lightning Source LLC
Chambersburg PA
CBHW022051080426
42734CB00009B/1302